ACRONYMS
TO
LIVE BY

Ratoeba Piet Ntema

ISBN: 0620749113
ISBN-13: 978-0620749114

DEDICATION

To:_____________________

____

____

____

____

____

____

____

From:_________________

Date:

ACKNOWLEDGMENTS

I acknowledge the highest power from
God.

In your **LANE** you...
L learn to
A accept who you are;
N nurture and
E empower yourself.

FAIL is...
F false
A actions
I interfered with
L life.
...we can always come back
and start again and push for
our success.

TIME is a....
T true & tough
I instrument used to
M manage
E everything & everyone.

LOVE...
L look
O only for
V valuable things in
E each other.

LOVE...
L live
O openly and
V value
E everything and everyone.

LOVE ...
L live
O orderly,
V vividly,
E encouraged.

LOVE...
L let each
O one of you
V value
E everything and each other
in your relationship.

LIVE is...
L Look
I inherent and
V value
E everything & everyone.

PATIENCE is about...
P planning
A acting
T timing
I involving
E engaging
N nurturing
C consulting
E encouraging.

HATE is the...
H highest
A activity of
T truly being
E enslaved.

HATE...
H has
A a way of
T trapping and troubling
E everyone having it.

SMART is...
S sexy
M matured
A attractive
R real and
T talented.

GYM for some stands for...
G getting
Y yummy by
M moulding the body.

BLESSER is....
B being a
L loser in
E everything
S smart people
S strive to
E earn and
R retain.

FAKE is...
F false
A activities that try to
K keep
E everyone entertained.

WORDS can....
W weigh
O others
R rapidly
D down if not
S selected carefully.

The **TRUTH** is....
T telling it as
R real as it is and
U understanding
T the
H hurt it can bring.

DEATH...
D destroys
E everything/everyone
A around us and it
T touches our
H health so bad.

I urge you, to always refer to
YOURSELF as....
Y young,
O outgoing,
U unstoppable,
R real,
S smart,
E energetic, and
L living
F fully.

SUCCESS is being…
S smart and
U understand that, you
C can
C care;
E empower; and
S support others to
S succeed too, without you
losing a thing.

WORK...
W when
O others
R rest, you
K keep on going.

When it feels **HARD**, it
simply means....
H have it
A anyway,
R regardless of the
D difficulties.

OPEN minded person is....
O one
P person whom
E everyone
N needs.

PULL in life means...
P people
U understand
L little about
L life. That's why challenges
pull us down so easily. We
take life for granted.

___

When you are **SAD**, it is
actually the right time to...
S seek an
A angelic
D direction.

Your time is **WASTED**...
W when your
A actions are not
S supported by
T talent,
E energy,
D determination and
dedication.

Feeling **COLD** is like
hearing more of this
statement:
C cuddle with the
O one you
L love
D deeply.

To **HUSTLE** is more like
to...
H hunt
U until
S something
T tangible and
L large
E emerge.

SEX...
S slow
EX exemption of love, if it is
good.

SEXY…
S smart
EX exquisite and
Y yummy.

QUICKIES....a man is
Q quickly
U undressing an
I individual without
C caressing;
K kissing; or
I intriguing, before
E entering her
S sexually.

DREAMS...
D direct
R right
E energy into
A actions,
M motivation and to
S success.

When they **GLOW** in the
morning, it is because they...
G got
LO loved
W wildly.

In the **MORNING**....
M many
O of us
R regain
N new,
IN intriguing
G goals.

Every **MORNING**...
M move
O on and
R realise
N new
I interesting and
N normal achievable
G goals.

With **GOD** by your side you simply...
G go
O on to your
D destiny.

It is by **GRACE**.....
G God
R rebuilds,
A approves,
C cares, and
E empowers his people.

GRACE...
G God loves us,
R regardless of who we are, he
A accepts us, he
C cares about us and he
E empowers us when we are weak.

To **IMAGINE** your great
ideas is more like...
I Implanting
M Moulding
A Activating
G Generating
I Involving
N Nurturing
E Engaging ...before you can
get to the end result of your
ideas.

FEAR....makes
F few to
E engage in
A activities that
R reward.

What are your **FEARS** mean
to me...
F For as long as
E everyone is
A accepting and agreeing
with your
R reality you will be
S sucked into your comfort
zone and you wouldn't want
to disappoint anyone.

When they say they are
FINE it simply means...
F first
I interrogate them and
N nurture the situation and
E empower them.
Many people would just say
they are **FINE** trying to
avoid the explanation of
what is actually wrong.

BITCH stands for…
B beautiful;
I inspirational;
T trustworthy;
C courageous and
H helpful.

WHORE …
W woman who
H happens to make
O other women
R realise their
E emptiness without their
men.

A **WOMAN** should be the....
W wealth
O of her
MAN.

WAITING...
W while
A acting
I in
T the
I interest of
N nurturing
G good.

RUMOUR...
R rubbish
U used to
M mix up
O original
U untold
R reality.

PARENT...

P please
A accept
R responsibility and
E encourage; empower; and
N nurture
T those talents.
Being a PARENT doesn't necessary mean you know all or more and you cannot listen to your children. Remember there are no qualifications for being a parent. No manual is coming with a BABY. LEARN to LISTEN.

KISSES...
K keep
I individuals feeling
S secured;
S supported;
E encouraged and
S smiling.

PAIN....
P put us
A all
I in a
N new perspective.

PAIN is...
P pressure
A acting to
I instil
N new action.....
Let your PAIN benefit you
in all aspect, if not it will kill
you.

CHURCH should...
C care for;
H help;
U uplift;
R rebuild/revive;
C cultivate;
H heightens its members.

At **HOME** you are...
H harmonized
O organized
M moulded
E encouraged and
empowered.

HOME is...
H highly
O organized
M moulding
E environment.
Go HOME as often as you
can when life seem to trouble
you.

FRIENDS...

F find
R real
I individuals who will
E encourage; empower;
N nurture;
D develop and
S support you.

TEARS...

T to
E everyone who is
A always hurting others, you will
R reap what you
S sow on day.

R.I.P...

R rest assured that all
I individuals will
P pay for what they have
done.

ANGER...

A activates
N new
G grinding
E energy for
R real when it is directed
properly.

ANGRY…
A annoyed
N negative
G grumpy
R rebellious
Y yank.

May **LIFE...**
L let
I individuals at least
F feel the
E excitement & enjoyment
of being alive!!!

WISH...
W wisdom,
I intellect and being
S smart doesn't just
H happen.

FAME...
F false
A actions/activities
M manipulating
E everyone.

I don't explain my **NO**. My
NO means…
N not
O open for discussion.

To **DICK** is to...
D develop an
I insight;
C clairvoyance and
K kindness.

GREAT is ...
G getting
R real in
E every
A action you
T take.

HUMANS should be…
H helpful
U understanding
M mindful
A accepting
N natural and
S supportive.

POWER is …
P people
O of
W wealth
E empower and
R revive; rebuild others.

Being **MATURED** is...
M meeting
A actions
T that
U unsettle you, but still
R remain
E encouraged and
D determined.

DADS should...
D do
A all the
D duties that
S support their kids.

FATHER …
F frequently
A acting
T to
H help
E everyone to achieve
R regardless.

NAKED is …
N none
A attractive and it
K kills and
E extinguish
D desire.

FEMALE is being...
F fabulous
E exquisite
M marvellous
A angelic
L loving
E entertaining.

Getting **SICK** is a way...
S Satan
I is
C checking your
K kicks/knocks.

SAD is...
S surely
A advancing the
D devil.

Being a **LADY** is...
L looking
A attractive from
D deep inside
Y you.

When you **HELP** you…
H heightens
E enlightens
L loves and
P protects.

Being **HAPPY** you...
H hold on to the
A activities that
P put less
P pressure on
Y your life

POSSIBLE simply means...
P people
O of
S success,
S succeed
I intensively
B because
L living life has
E empowered them.

WRONG is...
W waiting
R restlessly
O over
N nothing
G good.

POTHOLES are...
P pain & pressure
O of all
T times
H hanging
O over your
L life to
E enslave and
S slow you down.

SELFISH is...

S self
E empowering
L life that
F fulfils the
I interests of a
S smart
H human!!!

REAL MAN is...

R reliable,
E encouraging,
A accepting,
L loving and
MAN manageable.

PUSH…
P preparation
U under
S stress
H helps.
There is never the right time
to prepare!!!

My **MOM** is...
M mentor
O of
M mentors.

MENTORS are...
M motivating
Encouraging/empowering N
nurturing
T training
O organizing and
R reforming
S structuring!

Do you **CUM**?
C cultivate
U understanding that
M mould your mind?

My **STAR** is...
S smart
T talented
A artistic and
R remarkable.

DIG is...
D Doing
I intensively
G good.

GAME is...
G getting into
A actions that
M mould and
E empower.

FAT is…
F fabulous,
A attractive and
T tough...
Beauty comes from within.
Feel good about your size.

HEAT is...
H Hell
E encouraging one to
A act
T tough.

SINGLE...
S showing
I interest, but
N not
G getting
L love and
E entertainment

STORM...
S some
T times,
O one is
R reformed
M massively.

FAITH is...

F forever
A acting with the
I intentions
T to
H have.

DEATH is...

D doing
E everlasting
A action of taking us
T to
H heaven.

With **GIFT**...
G Go
I invest and
F further your
T talent.

My **RISE** has...
R radically
I inspired
S someone to
E escalate.

My **CRUSH** is...
C cute
R radiant
U understanding
S smart, Sexy
H humble.

When I **ADMIRE**!! I....
A add
D determination;
M motivation;
I inspiration and
R rapid
E empowerment.

THANKS...

T the
H humbling
A acts
N never
K kill the
S smiles.

PLEASE…

P people
L like
E everyone to
A ask
S someone to
E expense on their behalf.

Change of **MINDSET**
means…
M move
I in a
N new
D direction that is
S suggesting an
E effective
T throughput.

He is **GREAT**!! Meaning...
He...Guards
He...Reforms
He...Empowers
He...Advocates
He...Transforms

I **GOT** you…
G God
O of all
T Times

Have **ORDER** in your life…
O organize
R rebuild
D date/decorate
E empower
R revive.

GIRL...

G gorgeous
I Intrinsic
R real
L loving

Be your **BEST** and do your
BEST, for the BEST...
Which means to be…
B beautiful
E en-courageous
S smart
T talented.

PROBLEM…
P plain
R robbery
O of
B beautiful
L life
E experimenting
M moment

Dear Self, today you are
going to **SHINE...**
S smile
H help
I inspire
N nurture
E encourage.

In a **NEW YEAR**…
N never
E entertain
W what
Y you've
E encountered
A as
R rubbish in a previous year.

Not everyone will stay in
SOBER meaning…
S staying
O organized
B bright
E enlightened
R real.

A man and woman should
form a **TEAM** because…
T together
E everyone
A achieve
M massively.

Being **HAPPY**, you…
H hold on to
A activities that
P put less
P pressure on
Y your life.

To **STUDY** is to get...
S smarter
T transformed
U understanding
D developed
Y young again

SUICIDE...
S some times
U under a lot of pressure an
I individual
C can
I intentionally
D decide to
E exit his or her life.

PRIDE is that...
P pressure that is
R residing
I inside an individual and
D destroying
E every second chance one
could/might have.

PEACE …
P people should
E encourage
A acts of
C caring and of
E empowerment.

SEPTEMBER people are...
S special,
E elevated
P people who are
T trying their best in
E every hour of the day, who
are
M making new friends, new
heights and
B being good in making
E exciting discoveries, and
they are
R reliable.

I refers to **MYSELF** as:
M masculine,
Y yummy,
S smart,
E elegant,
L loving and living
F fully

I regard **YOU** as...
Y young,
O outgoing and
U unstoppable.

I am **RICH**...
R real,
I independent,
C courageous, and
H humble.

A **LIAR**....
L lives as
I if
A all is
R real.

DEBT...
D deteriorates
E everything you got and it
B brings
T troubling times to life.

HUGS…
H he who
U understands
G gets to
S support more.

GREED makes one to…
G get
R rid of
E everything or
E everyone just to fulfil this
D desires.

Before you **JUDGE** me...
J just
U understand my
D demons and
G get me
E empowered.

GOALS make you...
G get
O out there to
A act; to
L live and to
S succeed.

When you have **GOALS**,
you...
G go all
O out
A and make your
L life a
S success.

When you **FOCUS,** you...
F find
O optimal
C concentration and
U understanding of being
S smart and successful.

I was told to be **HUMBLE**
all the time, meaning to...
H humanly
U understand
M my
B being with its
L limitation and seek for
E empowerment.

TOUGH is....
T trying
O out everything in my
disposal
U until I
G get what I have worked
H hard for.

You get **TIRED** when you

have...

T tried everything

I in your power and nothing

is

R really coming your way and

E everyone is expecting you

to

D do everything by yourself.

All women should have
BREASTS...
B be
R realistic
E enthusiastic
A attentive
S smart
T tough and
S succeed.

All Men should have
BALLS...
B be
A aspirants
L lovers
L listeners and
S smart to succeed.

Before people **FUCK**, they...
F first do foreplay,
U undress each other,
C cares each other as they
K kiss

"being **WET**..." it means....
W when are you
E entering my
T tunnel?

A **NIGHT** is...
N never
I interesting without a
G good and a
H hot company
T to be with.

Being **PATIENT**, you...
P pay
A attention
T to time as an
I individual and you
E encourage yourself
N not
T to give up.

PROMISE...
P puts
R rise to
O our
M minds and
I intrigue a
S sense of
E expectation.

When you feel **ALIVE,**
you...
A allow and
L let only
I individuals who are
V valuable to
E enter your life.

HOPE…
H has a way
O of
P putting
E everyone on a forward
movement.

CHEATING...

C creates
H havoc to
E everyone who is
A acting
T towards
I intriguing and
N nursing the
G good feeling it brings
initially.

The **HURT** will...
H humble you
U until you are
R really and
T truly healed.

We **WAKE UP**...
W when
A all we cared for and failed
to
K keep is out there
E everywhere
U unshaped, unrecognized
and
P perishing.

We need to **TALK** statement
simply means...come and...
T take
A all that
L life let us have and
K keep it as your memory.

JOBS are...

J just
O opening the
B business in employees,
while the employer is
S seriously making more
wealth.

STRESS...

S speaks
T the truth about the
R reality
E everyone ignores and
S struggles to deal with it,
while they
S silently die from the inside.

When you are not in a
RACE with others, you...
R rebuke and
A activate the power to
C cancel anything negativity
and
E empty it out of your life.

———————

Most people who made a
MISTAKE before are...
M matured
I individuals who are
S smarter;
T thornier;
A alert;
K keen and
E established.

When you feel **TIRED** of
trying to change your
situation, it could probably
means it is...
T time to let God's
I intervention to
R restore and
E empowers you as he
D directs your life.

TEACHERS...
T try their best to
E empower,
A assist,
C coach learners and
H harness an
E environment that is
R really
S suitable for learning.

Every man who is seen as a
TRASH can be...
T transformed;
R reformed
A altered; alleviated;
S shaped;
H heightened.

In **BED** you will...
B be
E entered so
D deeply.

As you **RISE** up from your
bed today...
R realize your
I individuality and
S start
E empowering yourself

When you are **NICE**...
N not every
I individual will
C care or
E embrace that.

When you **BRAG,** you...
B boast about things that are
not
R really going to be
A around for long before
they are all
G gone or you are gone.

When she says she is
HORNY, she simply
means....
H humbled
O organized
R realistic
N new and
Y young.